Dr. R. Henry Migliore

COMMON SENSE MANAGEMENT

MANAGEMENT

AN

ACCOUNTABILITY
A P P R O A C H

COMMON-SENSE MANAGEMENT
An Accountability Approach

by
R. Henry Migliore
Professor of Strategic Planning and Management
Northeastern State University/University Center at Tulsa

ISBN 0-89397-402-1
Copyright © 1990 by
R. Henry Migliore
Managing for Success
P.O. Box 957
Jenks, Oklahoma 74037

Illustrations by Mike Kelly

Published by
Nichols/GP Publishing
11 Harts Lane
East Brunswick, NJ 08816

Table of Contents

Acknowledgements

Thanks to Elaine Drain for typing the manuscript and the late Lynn Nichols who edited the original versions. Thanks also to Purolator Products for funding my position and providing resources so the book could be completed.

H. Migliore

Part I:
Foreword/Review/Introduction

Foreword

Through the years, I have had the opportunity to work with many organizations conducting seminars and workshops in every area of the country. In addition, I have taught 20 years of undergraduate and graduate classes. A key driving force for me has been the ministry of helping people to develop, teaching them to find solutions for their problems, and to become better managers in every aspect of their lives.

To this end, in my teaching and writing I always relate academic and business principles to things with which they are easily related.

On one occasion at a seminar in Nebraska, I was drawing a diagram to illustrate the "lawn mowing theory" when a participant asked, "Why don't you write all this up?" A few years later, here it is ..... Common Sense ..... (in) ..... Management. Then I could see that the greatest book ever written, the Bible, also lent itself to common sense.

I must acknowledge that about half of these topics are not original. The Care and Feeding of the Boss, Lawn-mowing Theory, Iceberg, Stinger, etc. are all mine. In the latter part of the article are items taken from Kalin Dahl, and others came from sermons, speakers, and various other sources.

R. Henry Migliore
Summer 1990

Review
by Norma Jean Lutz

Dr. Migliore, Professor of Strategic Planning and Management, Northeastern State University/ University Center at Tulsa, has put together a book of pithy and thought-provoking vignettes. It is aimed at management and labor, but many points are applicable to all facets of life.

Under the topic, "Pay Me Now or Pay Me Later," he teaches: "My basic routine when I went into a new job was to discuss, 'Here's what we are going to do; here's where we are going, and if you have a problem, let's get it resolved now.' In short, get the issue out on the table right at the beginning."

This type of action can be applied to many situations where communication is at a premium.

Because of Dr. Migliore's expertise in the area of business and management, experience is the note that rings through the pages of this book. The accompanying cartoons lend life to each short teaching.

Some of the teachings, perhaps due to familiarity with the subject matter, could use more explanation and clarity; some examples seem to be too weak to carry the point of the lesson, but this would be easily taken care of in editing.

It is my thought that many of these concepts are never taken into consideration by businesses; such as "The Care and Feeding of the Employee": "the second day on the job, begin training your replacement."

There have been many books on success, management, time management, etc., but this book is unlike any of them because of the short snappy examples (lessons, or whatever) that make for quick, easy reading.

The easy-to-read concept tends to widen the market out from the business world to many other areas where people must deal with other people.

Introduction

Managers often tend to take themselves too seriously and to complicate matters instead of keeping them simple.

Henry Migliore has avoided both of these tendencies in this easy-to-read and insightful book. He delivers the message but succeeds in doing so without the excess of verbiage which often accompanies the subjects about which he writes.

The reader is tempted to read the entire book at one sitting. This could be a mistake! Each "gem" in the book is one that should be read, thought through, and then digested for later application.

While Common Sense Management is an approach most of us advocate, many times there is an uncommon lack of it.

Dale D. McConkey
Professor of Management
School of Business
University of Wisconsin-Madison

Part II:
Practical Applications of
Common Sense Management

Care, Feeding of a Boss

Care and Feeding of the Boss

Almost everyone has a boss — someone who oversees and is responsible for one's activities and output. Sometimes unfortunate communication gaps exist between the boss and subordinate. Many well-managed organizations are finding various ways to close these gaps. Every person should take the time to determine what the boss expects in specific, measurable terms.

An exercise often used in different settings is to ask a boss and subordinate to list the five most important results expected by the subordinate. Let's examine a typical case. Between 50 and 60 percent of the items on the lists of the persons assembled are not in agreement. It's revealing to go through that exercise yourself. I've run this exercise many times, and I have never had a group that had more than about a 60 percent agreement. Since this is true, that means half of the things people in organizations are working on are things the boss doesn't rate as important. I think that's at the root of most of management's problems. The "care and feeding of the boss theory" suggests that you make up the expectation list and then reach agreement before starting. It does not make sense to work on something if you don't know where you're going, what's expected, or even what is most important. The boss is "fed and happy" when he knows you agree on what is to be done and when. He is even happier when you get the desired results.

The key issue, as we all care for our bosses is to be accountable and responsible. The theory encourages

Employee Care, Feeding

the subordinate to report progress even if the boss doesn't ask for it. I'm continually surprised at the number of organizations and the people in them that seem to work on a day-to-day basis. Everyone assumes everyone else knows what to do. Take action — care and feed your boss!

Care and Feeding of the Employee

You can initiate the same "feeding of the boss" process with the persons working for you. They prepare a list of what they believe they are to accomplish. You prepare a similar list. Then compare lists and negotiate. The way to get along with people is to determine what the key end result is going to be, and a lot of other problems will take care of themselves. Expectations must be communicated and known in advance. A key to successful "care and feeing" is giving the employee timely feedback on performance. Constantly reinforce positive results and coach, correct, and discourage negative results.

We have been doing a series of studies on people's attitudes about their jobs and work environments for over 10 years. Those respondents that indicated they were unhappy with their jobs also indicated they were unclear of job goals, didn't receive feedback on performance, and didn't know how they stood with the boss. The reverse was true of those that were happy on the job. They had clear goals, negotiated with the boss, and had a regular system of review. It's important to care for and to feed your employees.

Iceberg Theory

Iceberg Theory

An organization, in many ways, can be likened unto a vessel crossing the North Atlantic. If you've ever studied icebergs, you know that only a small part of the iceberg is above the water. You cannot see what is under water. An organization, like a ship, is going somewhere. In most cases, the organization and the ship have a target, profitability in a certain market or a distant port. Both are intent on survival. You want all hands on deck. You want a systematic way to be alert for the icebergs. Actually, anyone can see an iceberg. The janitor, a salesman, or anyone on that ship might be able to spot the iceberg.

Strategic Planning/MBO (SLRP/MBO) by its very nature encourages the communication process. It gets everybody in tune with what the organization is doing. It gets all hands on deck watching for icebergs. A shipmate sees the iceberg, sounds the warning, goes to upper management — the captain of the ship — who studies the problem, sees the iceberg, and sees that the course of the ship can be turned because of what the lowest-level member of the organization has seen. The same thing has happened in organizations I have worked with. A salesman noticed a new use for his company's product out in the field. He saw competition beginning to notice the same thing. Since we had set up a procedure to send information back, R&D got hold of it. Suddenly, everybody in the organization is helping to get somewhere. The company made a fast entry into a new market.

If a company is going to achieve its goals, it must have a continuous flow of information coming from all

21

Promotion Theory

areas of the organization. The system of management that best achieves this is the SLRP/MBO system whereby information is constantly being collected and sent upward in the hierarchy.

Promotion Theory

The first advice I received when I went to work at Continental Can Co. was, "if you really want to get ahead in business, the second day on the job, begin training your replacement." I always wondered about that. I didn't see the point until I had worked in organizations for a number of years. If you are going to get ahead and be promoted, you have to develop someone to take your place. This lesson I learned when a manager friend was passed over for a promotion. A few years later I understood why he was passed over. It would have weakened the organization. If the company had promoted him, no one was available to take his place. He had not used what I call "care and feeding of the employee."

It's your job to develop people and to get started developing them fast. If you are the only person who can do a particular job, and a promotion comes along, you will be passed over. Your boss might say, "gosh, you would really be good at this, but what's going to happen — no one's trained to take your place." Many times, people are so protective on the job that they don't share and help people develop. They're afraid that "if I train that person, then he will get my job, and I'll be jobless." SLRP/MBO makes you focus on the people who are working for you, to develop them by setting objectives, and to assist them in meeting their objectives.

Managing's Like Parenting

Managing's Like Parenting

Management and rearing children have much in common. I have personal experience in both arenas for about the same period of time. Everyone believes he can do a good job until he tries it. It has taken me this long to see this theory because of experience with our children. Being a parent is the most difficult task I ever faced. "Deaning," teaching, consulting, writing are relatively easy. But rearing children is a difficult undertaking. Parents don't really receive any formal training. They just go through an evolutionary process. As children keep growing, parents don't recognize the changes; they do the best they can, but they really have little insight as to changes taking place in the children's lives.

I've noticed the same process in management. The organization grows through highly predictable stages. It appears that most managements are not interested in receiving training; the only time they do is when disaster strikes. As a consultant, I usually don't get called in until deep trouble looms.

A large oil company asked me to come in and work with its management team. After a single day's stay, I told the chief executive officer, "As well as things are going, I haven't figured out what you want me for. It looks to me as though you have a fairly good management system, and things are going well." His response was part of what I am trying to get across here. He said, "We want to do better; we don't want to relax; we think we can raise productivity and manage even better." This theory suggests management and parenting have common problems. In both cases, management development and training makes the task easier and the organization more efficient.

Stinger Principle

Stinger Principle

The "Stinger Principle" was inspired by bees. If you don't let people know that things are not going as they should, they tend to be uncertain, experience anxiety, and do not to perform as well. The Stinger Principle works after the setting of objectives, working hard, rewards if we meet them, and getting an appropriate stinger if the objectives are not met. The well-placed stinger gets our attention.

For example, here are the key, specific, measurable things that a boss ought to do: Periodically review how well the person is doing, and if things aren't going as they should, then the stinger should be applied. What happens in organizations is that some persons get very high ratings or no performance feedback at all, and then, suddenly, they are fired or replaced. The organization doesn't have a clear, candid appraisal system. If a person is off target, he should get a stinger as a signal to get back on target.

The legal system is beginning to take exception to this. In performance appraisal, one tends to gloss over things; to say, "Hey, Fella, you're doing just fine, we appreciate your hard work, and it's good you showed up for the company picnic; you did well in our golf tournament," but never getting down to brass tacks. What did you agree was to be accomplished and did he do it? And if he didn't do it, then you have to apply the stinger. "Okay, Fella, here's what was expected on the job; you have not accomplished the key results; you're going to have to adjust your performance." I believe people want to know where they stand. Only by knowing where they stand can corrections be made and thus assure a better chance of success. SLRP/MBO, with its regular review, provides the opportunity for praise or the stinger.

Cycle Theory

Cycle Theory

I began to notice that in athletics, business, and organizations things tend to run in cycles. Let us consider trends in basketball. When I was in junior high, I remember reading about St. Louis University, Eddie Hickey, and the battle for the Missouri Valley Conference basketball title. In 1954, Oklahoma A & M had Bob Kurland, and Oklahoma City University had Hub Reed. If you are an ardent basketball fan, you know that during 1984, St. Louis University and Oklahoma City University were both at a low ebb. Who would have believed in 1955, when it was highly ranked, that someday St. Louis University basketball would be in such a low spot a few years back in its quest for success? Now, both schools are back on top again. I've noticed the same thing in companies and organizations. In some ways, they tend to go through natural cycles. If you realize that, then as you start into a down cycle, you need to begin to be alert to management changes. A set of "flash points" should be set. The specific events that "flash" the downturn should be identified early. Most organizations hit bottom before reacting. Strategic planning will help you stay out of those cycles. Going through the steps of the strategic-planning process will help an organization see the start of a new cycle, and will help it react rather than go through the full length of the cycle.

Pay Me Now or Pay Me Later

Pay Me Now or Pay Me Later

I was reminded of this recently when an organization in deep trouble came to me with the plea: "You've got to help bail us out; you're the only one who can help." I couldn't help but recall that about 4 years ago, when the company was organizing, I was called in and asked, "We need some help getting started; we've heard of your reputation; will you help us?" I shared the process of strategic planning. I said, "Here's what you've got to do to set up an organization to run consistently."

And the president said, "No, I don't have time for that. You mean take 6 weeks to set an overall plan and have committees work on the purpose of the organization? We've got to get going; we've got to get in the marketplace; we'll set the plan and hire the people and get going."

The "Pay me now or pay me later" theory means that you have to take the time to get people involved — set up the plan. If you don't, you'll pay for it later. There are no shortcuts to good management and planning. This organization right now has almost reached the point that it's doubtful that it will survive. Its leader is anguished and floundering. It would have been an insurance policy to have gone through the process properly. The strategic-planning process is a must for any organized effort that is going to be successful.

Afraid to Fail

Anyone can walk a 2 x 4 plank on the ground for $100, but raise the plank 100 feet into the air, and there would be few takers. People are, by nature, afraid to take risks, afraid of failing. You can't develop to your potential without taking some risks. I know a youngster that dived off the high dive at a local pool all summer on frequent trips with his grandfather. One day his well-meaning mother was there. She was concerned and nervous, warning the child of all potential dangers. His next dive didn't go well and before long he completely stopped diving. This tendency to create a self-fulfilling prophecy contributes to our fear of failure.

Defensive End Theory

Defensive End Theory

In my football-playing days, I was a defensive end on an 8-3 formation and had one assignment — that was to hit the offensive end and then proceed to knock down everyone I could. I played 3 years of varsity football with this idea ingrained in my thinking. As I began to see how organizations operate, I began to see that if you spot problems, you have to confront them. When I spot trouble, rather than skirt it or shrug it off, or hope the issue will go away, I immediately round up the persons involved and go straight to the source of the problem with the zeal to resolve it.

The "Defensive End" theory says that if you spot trouble, go after it and solve it. As I worked my way through Continental Can and as I came into new jobs, one of the things I could always count on was that the union was, in most cases, there to oppose management. I began to notice that previous managers had always played the appeasement game. I don't mean to imply that I'm anti-union, because I'm not. Unions exist because management has not met its responsibility over a long period of time. If people are treated fairly, their needs met, and they have a sense of participation and well-being, they don't need a union.

If management doesn't accept its responsibility, then there is a legitimate need for people to unite. As I began to see how appeasement failed, my basic routine when I went into a new job was to discuss, "Here's what we are going to do; here's where we are going; and if you have a problem, let's get it resolved now." In short, get the issue out on the table right at the beginning.

Alamo Theory - - Toe the Line

Alamo Theory — Toe the Line

I've been using this philosophy since 1968. Here's where we are; here's where we're going; and here's the management system we are going to use. And I outline the strategic-planning SLRP/MBO concept. If you're with me, there's the line; step across, and here's how we're going to manage. If you don't believe in this management system, if there's a better way, then I'll help you find another job in the organization, another job somewhere else, or you'll be fired. I learned that lesson the hard way in a manufacturing assignment with my own management team. I'd gotten tough on everybody else and said "here's how we're going to do business." The company was going to close the plant if it didn't become productive. I began to notice that my whole management team was playing games with me. I was hearing everything I wanted to hear, but I wasn't seeing enough action. Let's face it — management resists change like everyone else.

Finally, I called a meeting on Saturday, let my blood pressure mount as high as I dared, and we just had it out. I said, "Look, I'm clearing the decks. You guys will not be here next week if you don't get on the stick. Here's how we're going to manage; here's how we're going to do it. Are you with me?" That got their attention, and from then on the story was that of a dramatic turnaround, very profitable, which helped turn around a bad situation. You've got to get people with you, and by meeting your problems head-on and explaining to them how you are going to manage, I think you are in better shape to assure success.

Lawn Mowing

Lawn Mowing

The total organization objectives can be described as a lawn in need of care. The purpose is to get the lawn in tiptop shape within a certain time. Every worker (in the case of organizations, the management team) looks at the total job to be done and, based upon strengths, weaknesses, and experience, divides up the work. It is like a crew of workmen looking at a yard in need of attention. Objectives and tasks are set before the work starts. When everyone knows the end results to be achieved, the work begins. Too many organizations go to work with no plan, no direction, and people uncoordinated. There is a mentality in these organizations that there is a noble courage to laugh and let things work out as you go. There is a high cost in this management style — much waste and confusion. The lawn-mowing theory encourages looking at the total task; dividing up the work; deciding the best, most economical way to do it; and then going to work. The people doing the work feel better because they know where they are going and tune in on the plan.

Are You Always Right?

Are You Always Right?

People frequently ask me this. My wife and children rejoice in those instances when things don't turn out as I predict. Tony Andress, a veteran manager with Continental Can Co., helped my wife, Mari (8+ months pregnant with our daughter Theresa at the time) into a chair at a company party in 1966 and said, "Henry has wild ideas, and they always seem to work." I'm really not all that sharp, but I do my homework and study the basics. If I see that people are not being involved in planning a project, and they are a key to making the project a success, it is easy to predict "this project won't be successful, and people will be unhappy in 6 months." There is a set of basics that you cannot violate. If you do, the results are predictable. We do not take advantage of what we already know.

A good example is the case of Thomas Edison, the nineteenth century's most successful inventor. Most academic historians agree that he so totally mismanaged the businesses he started that he had to be removed from each one so they could be saved. Books are full of similar stories. The person that starts something has trouble managing it after it begins to grow. It doesn't take a genius to see a like situation and predict trouble is coming. All kinds of things are predictable if we study the basics and then adjust the plan accordingly.

Subway

Subway

Once you get something started, for example a new product or service in a business, it is like a New York subway — you can't get off when you want to. My sister, Mary Helen, and I discovered this fact of life as we missed a stop and headed on toward Brooklyn. If you don't check the route, you don't even know where you are going. The key issue is to do a good job of planning and know in advance where you can get off if things don't go as expected. Some people get on for the ride, don't know where they are going, and don't know how to get off. The "get-off" plan is as important as the "get-on" plan. A contingency plan is needed, along with asking a large number of "what if" questions anytime something is started or before getting on for the "ride."

View World with Colored Glasses

View the World Through Colored Glasses

I remember the first time I field-dressed a deer on a hunting trip with a surgeon and a dentist as hunting companions. Since I am a results-oriented person, I just complete a job. Both of my companions were in a state of shock as I plodded through the chore. Their field of competence dictated precise cuts and careful cleaning. Different professions put high value on different things. We want others to see the priority of importance as we do. A pastor sees the spiritual base; a businessman looks to organized, results-oriented behavior; a dentist is interested in oral hygiene. We tend to see the world in the perspective of our own discipline. If we recognize this in advance, we can better understand others. Often, we don't understand why others don't see things as we do. If a person's orientation is not like yours, you can count on a different view and misunderstanding if you don't take the time to learn the other's perspective.

Stew in Your Own Juice

Stew in Your Own Juice

If people are not involved in the planning, it's your plan — not theirs. People will not "buy into" anything unless they have input. Whoever executes the plan must be involved in the plan. My strategic planning steps force this interaction. If you don't get everyone involved, your subordinates will let you "stew in your own juice." Organization veterans have perfected this strategy. The general feeling is to just go along with as little effort and support as possible.

Snowball

Snowball

Get some positive motion going, even if you must give it a push. At CCC Stockyards, the Press Manufacturing area had run in the red for 5 years. I came in mid-October 1967 and instituted SLRP/MBO, training programs, new preventive-maintenance programs, etc. That was the year Joe Namath said, "We will beat the Colts in the Super Bowl." People gave the Press Department about as much chance of running in the black as the Jets winning the Super Bowl. A theme was developed at CCC that we could do it and changed the view from negative to positive. After implementing Strategic Planning/MBO, we finally ran in the black. Once we did it, the "snowball effect" hit, and we were off and running with 10 straight weeks of top notch performance. Another example is Roger Bannister's 4-minute mile in 1954. Once the barrier was broken, others achieved the same result.

A manager is trying to create momentum out of what is sometimes a lifeless mess. Once started in motion, snowballs and organizations seem to move on their own momentum.

Get Your Head Above the Clouds

Get Your Head
Above the Clouds

Don't work day-to-day. Don't let the daily pressures dictate your actions. Get control by looking ahead. Get your head above the clouds and see where you are going. An airline pilot has radar and the tower to give him instructions in getting through the clouds. If he doesn't, he can become disoriented and even confused as to which way is up or down. An organization must get above the clouds and look out on the horizon to see where it is going. Some organizations and individuals go through their whole life spans going nowhere with no direction. This is the way we run many of our organizations — no direction, lost in the clouds. Strategic planning forces a view toward the future which then gives organization to the day-to-day tasks and decisions.

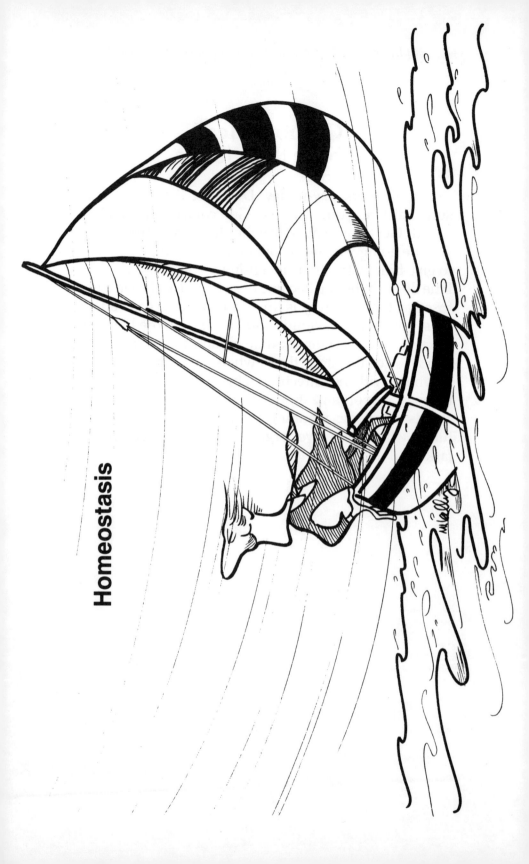

Homeostasis

Homeostasis

Homeostasis is a theory from the science of biology. One dictionary defines homeostasis as: "A relatively stable state of equilibrium or a tendency toward such a state between the different but interdependent elements of or groups of elements of an organism or group." The homeostasis theory of the firm suggests that the firm reacts to the outside environment and factors inside the organization and drifts toward a stable state of equilibrium. If this tendency does, in fact, affect organizations, management must recognize its responsibility to be sure the equilibrium reached is a positive, productive one. Sometimes I wonder just what effect management has over an organization over time. It appears to me that management is just along for a ride. It takes effort and a sense of conviction to force the organization to follow a positive track.

You could also call this the Thermostat or Thermometer Theory.

— A thermostat reads the temperatures/conditions/environment and adjusts the heater/or air conditioner to meet the desired temperature/ goal.

— A thermometer goes up and down with the temperature.

Seed Faith

Seed Faith

From Oral Roberts, President of ORU, this Biblical theory is derived from seed planting and harvests. As the farmer uses his best corn to plant the crop, he expects a good harvest. A person plants good seeds of deeds, love, friendship, and money and receives a great harvest from the Lord. A firm plants seeds of service to the community; a good employer pays taxes, makes a profit to ensure its long-term survival, provides a good product or service, acts in an ethical manner, and keeps the welfare of everyone in mind.

These good seeds planted will result in harvests of profit and a fair rate of return for investors.

Every time I have personally planted a seed of time, money, or prayer, it has returned as a harvest.

Natural Rhythm

Natural Rhythm

There is a natural rhythm to life. The tides, moon, and sun function on a natural cycle. There is a natural rhythm to living, interacting with society, our loved ones, spiritual life, and good health. All these factors must be in rhythm for a person to be successful.

Throughout my career, I have been associated with many "turnaround" experiences where poorly performing organizations have gotten their acts together and become successful. The first was Continental Can's No. 73 in St. Louis. That experience is documented in my book, *MBO: Blue Collar to Top Executive*. The latest has been Liberty Industries in Ohio. The methods in my books and articles seem to generate a natural rhythm. There is a rhythm to success. Although I find it hard to describe, there seems to be a "motion" or beginning spirit that must start for an organization to prosper. The combination of starting meetings, communication, and looking ahead all seem to get the motion started. Then a natural success rhythm begins — success is just around the corner.

"I'll Be True To You While You're Gone, Honey . . ."

"I'll Be True to You While You're Gone, Honey; Just Don't Be Gone Too Long."

This theme of a country/western song is the basis for good public relations. Identify the important people who impact your organization and be sure you personally interact with them on a regular basis. The interaction can be social, luncheon meetings, guest speaking, company picnics, etc. If you don't give them the personal touch, someone else will. Too often we seek someone only when there are problems. A relationship must be well established before trouble hits.

I have a practice that I have followed for years. I meet, correspond, and talk with all the people that are important to me. For example, Bobby Parker, Chairman of Parker Drilling in Tulsa, has encouraged me through the years. Recently, when my new book *Strategic Long-Range Planning* came out, I autographed a copy and hand delivered it to him. I said, "Thanks Mr. Parker..." and we chatted a few minutes. I could have mailed it to him and saved myself a lot of time. I appreciate him as a person and wanted him to know it.

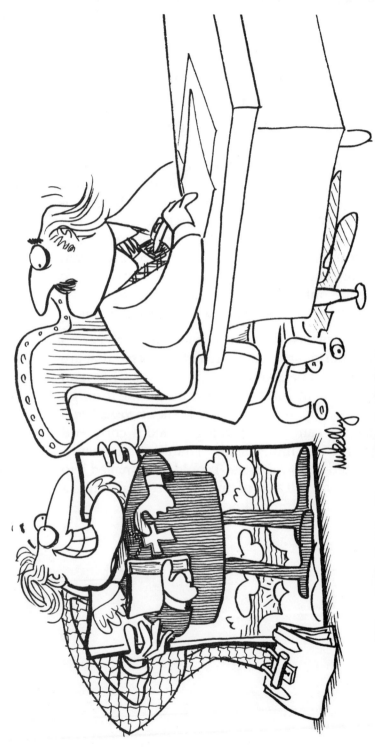

**Find Out He is a Christian by
How He Acts, Not by What He Says**

Find Out What Kind of Person He is by How He Acts, Not by What He Says

I have found that when a company or person uses a "good guy" orientation as a sales pitch, you can expect trouble is on the way. I would rather learn they are fine people by the way they do business and then have them tell me as a confirmation of what I already know. I have lectured on this point many times, often asking for a show of hands in the audience of those that have had the same experience. When I ask for those that have lost out on a business deal or transaction when the person or business made a point to stress the good guy dimension in the early part of the discussion, hands always go up.

I have found the same holds true for Christians. Watch out for the "talkers" and trust the "doers."

Get Out of the Ghetto

Get Out of the Ghetto

Analyze your strengths and strengthen your weaknesses. Find out what you do best and capitalize on it. If you don't like your station in life, go to work. Don't wait for a break; make the break happen. I have known many people who just sit back, talk a good game, and do nothing. Use your energy to make and carry out a plan, not to sit and complain about the situation. A significant amount of energy in America goes into complaining, criticizing, and not into changing the situation. After you do your best, you can ask God for His best. Many blacks use athletics to "get out of the ghetto." We all get imprisoned in a ghetto of some sort and must find a way out.

Be the Best You Can Be

Be the Best You Can Be

Don't worry about the other person. We spend too much time comparing ourselves with others. Class reunions turn out to be a time for comparison. Set realistic goals and compare your performance as you attempt to meet them. Be concerned with your own progress. Be the best you can be.

Never Give Up

Never Give Up

When I played basketball in high school for the Collinsville Cardinals, we were behind 7 points playing at Jenks with 19 seconds left. Somehow we tied the game and won. I will admit there was an element of luck, but we were pressing and playing all out to win. If we had given up, we would have lost. You are never beaten as long as you are trying to win.

Do It When It's Important

Do It When It's Important

Flowers before and after an anniversary make this point. After 20 years of marriage, if the flowers are there April 4, our anniversary is special. The timing is right. If they are presented in May, the opportunity is lost. If a person working for you does a good job or does something special, tell him right then, not later or, in some cases, not at all.

Success - Whole Person

Success — Whole Person

Success in life is based upon developing your own strengths to become what the Lord wants you to be. Success in all areas is what is important; spiritual, family, profession, health, and contribution to your fellowman. Too often we define success in terms of our career and financial goals. Set goals in other areas; vacations with family, helping others, reading books, etc. Be successful in all you do. I have known many successful career people whose personal lives are in shambles. Work had become almost a refuge to get away from their families. Although it isn't true in all cases, when I see someone on the job and working all hours, I suspect lack of fulfillment in other areas of life.

Be There in the Morning

Be There in the Morning

This theory — which emphasizes loyalty — is a key factor to success. It keys on dependability and trust. I have seen promotions go to less-qualified persons based on this key factor. Trust is important! I do not want anyone working for me who I do not feel is loyal to our mission and to me. Dr. Eugene Jennings of Michigan State, after a lifetime of studying careers, has reached this same general conclusion. Loyalty isn't something you can teach or perhaps learn. But be aware of this factor so you can better understand organization life.

We All Get in Trouble When We Get Too Fat

We All Get In Trouble
When We Get Too Fat

This theory applies to the human body as well as organizations. Overstaffing an organization is like being overweight — it slows you down. I notice that when my weight gets over 230 pounds, my blood pressure goes up, I tire easily, and don't have as much vigor. The same thing happens with organizations. Good objective setting with a hard look at results keeps an organization lean. Every resource must contribute to achieving key results.

Keep It Simple

Keep It Simple

We tend to make things too complicated. A few basics are keys to success in any endeavor. Lee Iacocca says that the keys to managing Chrysler are the letter of commitment and the quarterly review. Vince Lombardi, the legendary coach of the Green Bay Packers, listed three things:

1. You have to start by teaching the fundamentals. A player has to know the basics of the game and how to play his position.

2. You've got to keep the player in line. That's discipline. The men have to play as a team, not as a bunch of individuals. There's no room for prima donnas.

3. You've got to care for one another. You've got to love one another. Each player has to be thinking about the next guy. The difference between mediocrity and greatness is the feeling these players have for one another. Most people call it team spirit. When the players are imbued with that special feeling, you know you've got yourself a winning team.

If a few basic fundamentals are covered in any endeavor, it is likely to be successful.

Pine Tree

Pine Tree

After many hunting and fishing trips in the north woods, I began to reflect on the life cycle of many pine trees. Those that grow from a weak root system grow tall and then, by the weight of their own growth, topple.

People and organizations do the same thing. They grow fast without a solid foundation. Their own success and momentum actually create their own demise.

The solid foundation for an organization is based on honest dedication, belief in free enterprise, and a well-thought-out plan. I have seen people and organizations hit it lucky on timing in a market, product mix, or just plain being in the right place at the right time. They are convinced the success was based on their management insight and direction. They never really learn to plan or manage. Sooner or later, their own success creates a monster they cannot manage, and boom — they fail.

Failing to Prepare is Like
Preparing to Fail

Failing to Prepare is Like Preparing to Fail

The keys to sports success are preparation and practice. My coaches always said, "You will play like you practice." Thoroughly plan and prepare, and you are more likely to succeed. Without planning and preparation, you guarantee failure. I would rather overprepare with full planning and input from everyone than make a fast decision based on a few facts and emotion. Often, you save time in the short run only to find time is lost owing to costly mistakes in the long run. Proper planning is like buying insurance for success. There are always those little things that must be considered that affect the success of the venture.

Product Must Be Better Than
Sales Pitch

Product Must Be Better Than Sales Pitch

Oral Roberts used this phrase as part of a talk to a group of marketing managers attending an ORU School of Business seminar. He drew the analogy between the product he was selling, Jesus, the Christian walk, and business. The marketing managers must believe in their products in the same way. There is an underlying theme of honesty and integrity here also. The product or service must really help people and organizations meet their needs. When you believe in what you are selling, you can get excited. Too many times, the emphasis is on the sales pitch — get it sold and don't worry about the customer or consumer. A gaudy sales pitch creates expectations that, if not met by the product, create a dissatisfied customer — one who won't return!

The O-Ring

The O-Ring

Lee Iaccoca said it, and it continues to be painfully true. Success confirms what we already know, and the only way we learn is from failure.[1] The tragedy is that we're aroused only by gigantic failure and tragedy. We all learned from Nixon's resignation of the Presidency that if you make a mistake, admit it quickly. I'm calling this the "fess up" theory. If you've done a good job as a leader, your subordinates are going to understand and tolerate a few mistakes. Like everyone else, I make my share. What I am continuing to learn to do is to just say, "Well, I blew it on that one," make the proper apologies, if needed, and keep right on trucking.

Now we have the great tragedy of the shuttle disaster. What the task force found was a colossal failure of the management system. Fortune Magazine discussed NASA saying:

Top executives cannot afford to be isolated from the people below, who are in better touch with what is going on, and cannot afford to set unrealistic goals.

Yet not even this conclusion goes to the heart of the trouble at NASA. The flaw — call it an institutional virtue gone wrong — can trip many companies with overweening ambitions. In its widely hailed report on the tragedy, the commission headed by former Secretary of State William P. Rogers last month criticized "NASA's legendary 'can do' attitude." The agency, Rogers and his colleagues admonished, can't do everything.

Senator John Glenn went further. The can-do spirit, he noted, worked perfectly well in the old days, when it included a powerful commitment to safety. In Glenn's view, "can do" gave way over the years to "an arrogant 'can't fail' attitude." Managements assumed that no matter what risks they took, the shuttle would succeed.[2]

There must be a system of checks and balances, and a way to listen to the organization. I still remember an incident early in my career when I learned this lesson by accident and luckily didn't need a big failure to learn it. I was responsible for my company's industrial-engineering function at the time.

Working with Research and Development and corporate engineers, we had redesigned a system to handle the flow of liquids in the plant. It was an engineering marvel that was sure to bring me, at age 27, a fair amount of credibility when it worked properly and saved the company hundreds of thousands of dollars. The night before the big "launch," when we were to go over to the new system, I had come back into the plant and was nervously pacing the floor, looking things over. As I walked down one of the production lines, one of the night shift electricians walked by and sort of growled, "It'll never work." I thought, "What does that old goose know? Somebody ought to check his work record."

I continued walking down and started to get an uneasy feeling. I turned around, and since I didn't know his name, just hollered, "Hey, just a second." I still wasn't ready to admit he knew something that I didn't. After all, I had some talented people working for me. I asked him why it wouldn't work. He gave me a simple, direct, 60-second answer. I asked him why he hadn't said something months back, and his reply was "I quit making suggestions years ago when I noticed no one paid any attention. I could have saved this company thousands of dollars, but a person just tires of no one paying any attention." He then walked off into the shadows of the plant. I called my boss at home that night, incredibly embarrassed, but insisted that the startup on the new system couldn't go tomorrow and explained why. I assembled my staff the next morning and explained what the old electrician had shared with me. The room was quiet and all agreed, "He's right." We quickly redesigned and put a different component in the system, and though the startup was delayed, it was successful. I really learned a lesson on that one. At the time, at least, I thought I had, and it paid off again years later when I held a key manufacturing position.

The layout people had come up with a complete redesign of the manufacturing layout for the entire plant. They had been working on the project for months and had brought in outside architects, consultants, and others. When they made their final presentation, something clicked in my mind. I had approved it, my management team had approved it, but something said, "You had better ask the people." I told the lead presenter that if he would make the same presentation to a select group of maintenance people — electricians, truck drivers, and workers on the production line — and they approved it, then I would finally sign my approval.

A number of people in the room laughed, which made me more determined. I said, "No presentation, no signature," and that started some intellectual fisticuffs that nearly got out of hand. The next day we set up the presentation, and guess what? The 30-year grandmother type who had come into the plant to man the production line during the Second World War, and had stayed on through all the years, had a strange look on her face. Everybody was talking, but I could tell she wanted to say something.

I shut the rest of the room up and asked her what

she thought. She was so nervous she spoke hesitantly and had a little trouble getting started. She shared that the production line she was working on had been modified in the early '50s, along the lines of what the layout people were designing, and that the spoilage rate and downtime rate increased dramatically. She had worked on that line as a young woman and had had all kinds of difficulty keeping it open. The engineers and layout people said that just couldn't be, and let's get on with the show.

By then, my heels were dug in and I was ready for the fight. After we excused the people assembled, we had it out the rest of the afternoon. I told them I would not sign the final authorization until a study was done to see if she was right. Sure enough, she was 100 percent right and the entire project was scrapped. I'll never forget her coming by my office and meekly apologizing for stirring up trouble. I thanked her, assured her that I enjoyed conflict, and that she had done a great job and saved us a fortune.

This incident occurred in February 1968, and I have never consciously made a move of any importance without asking advice, approval, and recommendations from everyone around me, including the people who were doing the work.

I am amazed, as I work with organizations throughout America, to find management groups violating this principle. All you have to do is look at the unfinished highways, botched computer systems, empty stores, and wonder how many of these failures could be traced primarily to the very principles we're discussing here.

If America truly wants to compete on an international basis, we've got to quit giving lip service to how we use our most valuable resource — people. In spite of everything that's being written and said, the way we value, plan, and manage our most important resource in many cases is still getting lip service. Our economic future and, in many ways, the preservation of the society we live in, are going to be based on how we use our human resources. I'm hoping that it doesn't take a tragic failure to learn each one of the very simple principles of management. Equally important is controlling the arrogance that creeps into the executive suite. One thing the 1980s have taught us is that we can fail, and there is plenty of evidence around us to prove it.

---

[1] Lee Iaccoca, *Iacocca An Autobiography,* New York: Bantam Books, 1984.

[2] Burck, Charles E., *Fortune,* July 7, 1986. p. 8.

How You Use Today
Determines
How Tomorrow Uses You.

Make the most of each day you live.
Don't take anything for granted.
Be a good steward of the gifts God has given you.
Invest your time instead of spending it.
Along with challenges come new opportunities.

Be Content With What You Have
And Know What You Are.

Be satisfied with your possessions and belongings.

Don't let greed or jealousy creep in. Always strive to improve on qualities that will make you a better human being and a pleasant person to be around — courtesy, honesty, good-natured.

Three Kinds of People

People who *MAKE* things happen.
People who *WATCH* things happen.
People who *WONDER* "What happened?"

I believe God needs us to make things happen. That doesn't mean we don't pray, trust, and believe, because we do. It does mean we do our best and then ask God for His best.

You Win The Race With Heart.

Kentucky Derby — the horse runs out of oxygen
after the first mile, then wins on heart.
We all have talent, but the Christian should
always have heart.

Anger Is Just One Letter Away From Danger.

When you are angry, you are not as capable of making good decisions. Anything you say will likely come out wrong. Once something is said, you can't take it back.

If you don't know what you are talking about, keep your mouth shut.

The Best Kind of Pride Is That Which Compels a Person To Do His Very Best Work, Even If No One Is Watching.

Pride is a beautiful characteristic of human nature. It makes us feel good about ourselves. Every job you do is a reflection of yourself. The quality of your work speaks for you.

Unguided Missiles; Some Without Warheads

In this space age, I see many people zipping off here and there, always in a hurry but never really accomplishing anything. They remind me of a missile with no course. When they land, nothing happens. We all need a target, and when we hit it, something must happen.

If You Are Average, You Are As Close To The Bottom As You Are To The Top.

Most people want to stay in the middle of the pack. They might talk a good game but never put anything into their lives to move from average to excellent. God needs us to move to the top.

The Only Place Where Success Comes Before Work Is In The Dictionary.

There are no shortcuts to success. If you think you are going to be successful without good, old-fashioned hard work, you're only fooling yourself. Many people say to me, "Henry, you are so successful . . . things come so easy for you." That's not so. I have worked extremely hard all my life. My senior year in high school athletics is one example. I had a wonderful senior year, lettering in 4 sports, making all-conference in football and basketball. What most people didn't see was the years of running and catching passes after work with my friend and quarterback, Clay Lynch. I stayed after practice in basketball every day to shoot more baskets. The work paid off. Everything I have ever accomplished followed this same pattern.

The Indispensable Man

Sometime when you're feeling important;
Sometime when your ego's in bloom;
Sometime when you take it for granted,
You're the best qualified in the room.

Sometime when you feel that your going
Would leave an unfillable hole,
Just follow this simple instruction,
And see how it humbles your soul.

Take a bucket and fill it with water,
Put your hand in it up to the wrist;
Pull it out and the hole that's remaining
Is a measure of how you'll be missed.

You may splash all you please when you enter,
You can stir up the water galore;
But stop and you'll find in a minute
That it looks quite the same as before.

The moral in this quaint example
Is to do just the best that you can.

Be proud of yourself, but remember
THERE'S NO INDISPENSABLE MAN!

From The Lowest Depth There Is A Path To The Loftiest Height.

There is always a solution to every problem and every situation.

A Little Fellow Follows Me, I Dare Not Go Astray. For Which Direction I Shall Take, He'll Go The Self-Same Way.

In many ways the Fellowship of Christian Athletes follows this motto. The example set by athletes is followed by others. We all have the obligation to set a good example.

Clouds That Never Rain

Long-time friend, fellow faculty member, and fisherman, Chuck Farah, shared this with me. Many people are like clouds that drift in the sky but never really produce, as in the analogy, rain.

My Pal, R. G. Voight

...a great friend over the years, with whom I share a common birthday. All things work together for good, but not any one thing may be good. For example, the chocolate cake. The only thing that is good by itself is the glass of milk. Who would want to eat the flour, yeast, salt, raw eggs, bitter chocolate, or even the sugar? But, put them all together and they make a delicious cake.

The Final Mark Of A Successful Person Is Humility And How He Will Be Remembered.

The Mary Gladys Migliore Circle was formed in my home church, the Collinsville First United Methodist Church, after she passed away in 1972. She was a warm, loving, steady person. She was in many ways like the Biblical Andrew, a servant to all around her. Her memory lingers in so many hearts. A question all of us should ask ourselves is, "How will I be remembered?" I hope I can measure up to my wonderful mother.

Fess Up

Ever wonder what would have happened if former U.S. President Richard Nixon had quickly recognized the error of Watergate and immediately apologized for the actions?

Key Man

At the Indianapolis 500, there is always a big crowd and lots of excitement. The focus of attention is on the drivers. As I watched the 1967 race, I noticed that the man who puts the nozzle into the car and periodically fills it with gas was also a key person.

Teamwork

Jesus Christ fulfilled his mission on earth in 3 years. In those 3 years he poured himself into training 12 men. Those men followed up and have revolutionized the world. How much time do managers put into training, teamwork, and development?

Learn From The Mistakes Of Others — You Can't Live Long Enough To Make Them All Yourself.

I'm continually amazed at how we all fail to learn from our experiences. In the last 2,000 years, every conceivable mistake has been made and mankind continues making the same ones over and over. Case in point, as it relates to business: use of matrix organization structure in a large hospital.

I attended a professional meeting with a dinner speaker. He was a hospital administrator, and in his talk said, "And we will be using the matrix structure to get better results." My heart just sank. The matrix concept can work, but it is very complex, perhaps like flying a 747. Here was a growing piper club organization trying to fly a 747...doomed to failure. It was none of my business, but I met with the man later in his office and pleaded with him to be careful. As I predicted, it didn't work and caused havoc with lack of understanding, confusion, unclear responsibility, etc. I would call it a million dollar mistake!!

Do Not Learn The Tricks Of The Trade Before You Learn The Trade.

I understood this one when I started looking into the idea of investing in real estate. Tim Myllykangas, who I got to know at the 1985 Orange Bowl, is doing well in this business. His success is mentioned in the book entitled *Nothing Down*. He knows the "tricks of the trade" because he has invested the time and money to learn it. I have no business getting into real estate if I don't take the time to learn the trade.

Nobody Knows What He Can Do Until He Tries.

Dick Crawford felt he could be of service to the people and community of Tulsa, so he ran for Mayor in the 1985 election. Many people said his experience was limited. He won the election and took a shot at the job. He is doing an outstanding job during the difficult economic times facing the city and state of Oklahoma. He had the courage to try and it paid off.

Noah Did Not Wait For His Ship To Come In — He Built One.

Too many Christians are sitting on their hands waiting for God to act. We need to go into action. We do our best, then ask God for His best. Naturally we pray every step of the way, but the key is to do something.

The Difference Between Good and Great Is A Little Extra Effort.

In this competitive world, many organizations, churches, and people are good at what they do. It's the extra effort that helps achieve a higher level of excellence.

It Is Easier To Keep Up Than To Catch Up.

One bad habit many undergraduates get into is to let their college class assignments get behind and they "cram" for exams. I took the advice of Dr. George Gillen, the very popular business professor at Oral

Roberts University, and started giving pop quizzes to encourage the students to keep up in their work. I believe strongly that we all need to keep our priorities straight, work on what's important, and not fall behind.

Success Is Never Accidental.

You hear the "he's lucky" or "she got all the breaks" all the time. People make their own breaks. Success comes after hard work. I don't know of anyone who is successful that got there by accident.

The Fellow Who Is Pulling The Oars Has Little Time To Rock The Boat.

Have you ever noticed that the loudest complainers are usually the people not involved in the work. The key here is that a manager must involve key people in the plan and get them working on its execution. If I play a role or am "pulling the oars," I won't be "rocking the boat."

There Are No Second Chances For Making A First Impression.

People can only judge us by what they see, read,

and hear. The letter you mail, the way you answer the phone, and how you look all create an impression. That is a given you can't control. However, you can try to control what that impression is. A well-written letter, no errors on bond paper, a professional tone on the phone, and appropriate dress all help in making a good first impression. It's a fact that professional people conduct business over meals. I have seen people lose opportunities because of sloppy eating and dining habits.

Luck Is The Idol Of The Idle.

Too many people put too much emphasis on luck. Opportunities are created by opportunistic people. You can't sit back and wait for something to happen.

Never Ask Anyone To Do Something You Wouldn't Do Yourself.

The late Roscoe Henry Channing, for whom I am named, was President of Hudson Bay Mining and Smelting Company from 1927 to 1968. He graduated from Princeton University in 1889 as a mining engineer, was on the first all-American football team, and was a rough rider with Teddy Roosevelt. Based on society's measure of success, I believe he made it. Perhaps of equal importance was how he managed and dealt with people. He never asked a man to do anything he would not do himnself. It is said that after an explosion the miners were scared to go down and pick up the remains of a fellow miner blown to bits. Channing asked for volunteers — none coming forward. He, president of the company, got on work clothes and got a sack. He went 7,000 feet down in the mine by himself, picked up the remains, and brought it to the surface. He knew most of the 4,000 employees by their first names and had respect from his employees. There was only one strike in 30 years. He was ahead of his times, offering fringe benefits, free hospitalization, and vacations — things unknown in other mines at that time in Canada. He had flowers and plants in the mine building. It was a spotless building. The theory was that men spend 1/3 of their lives working, so why not give them pleasant surrounding to look. All of Channing's mines were the height of efficiency, always built on hillsides to take advantage of gravity to cut down the power usage. The mines never missed a dividend during R. Henry Channing's tenure.

Mother Theresa Says A Life That Is Not Dedicated To Service To Mankind Is Useless.

Interesting concept. IBM prominately uses the word service when discussing purpose and mission. The Lord has given all organizations and people certain gifts and strengths. If much is given, much is required. If we are all striving to serve mankind, the world can become a better place. We can all serve through our professions and our personal lives.

Working His Way Out of a Job

One good measure of the long-term effectiveness of a manager is the concept of working his way out of a job. This is done when key results are attained and the people in the work unit are performing. It is the ultimate test of delegation. In my entire career, the best example to date is Mr. Charles Triblcock, Chairman and President of Liberty Industries. Liberty is prospering, has a well-developed strategic plan, and a system developed to keep it on target. Liberty has a reward system that is tied to specific accountability of key results. Mr. Triblcock guides the organization even while away on annual European vacations, ski trips, and ten weeks in Florida. He is a role model for all of us.

Appendix
Other Quotes

REMEMBER THIS YOUR LIFETIME THROUGH —
TOMORROW, THERE WILL BE MORE TO DO...
AND FAILURE WAITS FOR ALL WHO STAY,
WITH SOME SUCCESS MADE YESTERDAY...
TOMORROW, YOU MUST TRY ONCE MORE,
AND EVEN HARDER THAN BEFORE.

—John Wooden

DO NOT LET WHAT YOU CANNOT DO INTERFERE
WITH WHAT YOU CAN DO.

IT DOESN'T MATTER WHERE YOU LIVE BUT HOW
YOU LIVE.

HE WHO KNOWS LITTLE SOON TELLS IT.

IF YOU ARE CONTENT WITH THE BEST YOU HAVE
DONE,
YOU WILL NEVER DO THE BEST YOU CAN DO.

THE MAN WHO HAS THE RIGHT TO BOAST
DOESN'T HAVE TO.

YOU DRIFT TOWARDS THE ROCKS, YOU ROW
TOWARD SUCCESS.

THE BEST PLACE TO FIND A HELPING HAND IS
AT THE END OF YOUR ARM.

A MAN HAS TWO ENDS — HEAD AND TAIL.
SUCCESS DEPENDS
ON WHICH HE EXERCISES MOST.

WHEN YOU'RE THROUGH IMPROVING, YOU'RE
THROUGH.

IF YOU DON'T KNOW WHERE YOU'RE GOING,
ANY ROAD WILL TAKE YOU THERE.

"NOTHING GREAT WAS EVER ACHIEVED
WITHOUT ENTHUSIASM."

—Emerson

TALENT IS GOD-GIVEN, BE HUMBLE.
FAME IS MAN-GIVEN, BE THANKFUL.
CONCEIT IS SELF-GIVEN, BE CAREFUL.

IF YOU THINK YOU ARE GOOD, THEN WHY NOT
BE BETTER?
IF YOU THINK YOU ARE BETTER, THEN BE THE
BEST.

WHATEVER IMPEDES A MAN, BUT DOES NOT
STOP HIM, AIDS HIS PROGRESS.

HAVING FUN IS DOING HARD THINGS WELL.

SET A GOAL — THEN GET RID OF THOSE THINGS
IN YOUR LIFE
WHICH KEEP YOU FROM ATTAINING THAT GOAL.

THERE IS JUST ONE DISCOURAGING THING
ABOUT THE RULES

OF SUCCESS — THEY DON'T WORK UNLESS WE
DO.

LINCOLN SAID, "I WILL GET READY AND THEN
PERHAPS
MY CHANCE WILL COME."

A STURDY OAK ISN'T GROWN IN A
GREENHOUSE.

CONSIDER THE HAMMER: IT DOESN'T LOSE ITS
HEAD
UNTIL IT FLIES OFF THE HANDLE.

YOU CAN NEVER WIN THE HEAVYWEIGHT TITLE
BY DOING
LIGHTWEIGHT EXERCISES.

THE LESS YOU TALK, THE MORE PEOPLE WILL
LISTEN TO WHAT YOU SAY.

A CHIP ON THE SHOULDER INDICATES WOOD
HIGHER UP.

THE TROUBLE WITH BEING A GOOD SPORT IS
THAT
YOU HAVE TO LOSE TO BE ONE.

IT TAKES 20 YEARS TO GROW AN OAK,
BUT ONLY 2 MONTHS TO GROW A SQUASH.

BEWARE OF A HALF-TRUTH — YOU MAY BE
GETTING THE WRONG HALF.

SUCCESS COMES FROM HANGING ON AFTER
ALL OTHERS HAVE LET GO.

A HARD FALL MEANS A HIGH BOUNCE IF YOU
ARE MADE OF
THE RIGHT MATERIAL.

EVEN A MOSQUITO DOESN'T GET A SLAP ON
THE BACK
UNTIL HE STARTS WORKING.

IT IS NICE TO BE IMPORTANT, BUT MORE
IMPORTANT TO BE NICE.

WHEN YOU GET TO THE END OF YOUR ROPE,
TIE A KNOT AND HANG ON.

WHEN YESTERDAY'S DEEDS STILL LOOK GOOD
TODAY,
THEN YOU HAVEN'T DONE MUCH TODAY.

GREAT MINDS DISCUSS IDEAS, SMALL MINDS
PEOPLE.

WHAT YOU ARE TO BE, YOU ARE NOW
BECOMING.

IT IS USUALLY UPHILL WORK THAT LANDS ONE
ON TOP.

ONLY THE PRESIDENT HAS NO CHANCE TO
ADVANCE

A MOB HAS MANY HEADS BUT NO BRAINS.

IF YOU DON'T KNOW WHERE YOU'RE GOING,
YOU'LL NEVER KNOW IF OR WHEN YOU GET
THERE.

FOREVER THE DREAM IS IN THE MIND,

REALIZATION IN THE HAND.

THE COURAGEOUS ARE THOSE WHO REACH.

I'M NOT WHERE I'M SUPPOSED TO BE,
I'M NOT WHAT I WANT TO BE,
BUT I'M NOT WHAT I USED TO BE.
I HAVEN'T LEARNED HOW TO ARRIVE;
I'VE JUST LEARNED HOW TO KEEP ON GOING.

THE HARDER YOU WORK, THE HARDER IT IS TO
SURRENDER.

THE HARDER YOU WORK, THE LUCKIER YOU
GET.

DON'T COUNT THE DAYS, MAKE THE DAYS
COUNT.

A PERSON IS NOT A FAILURE AS LONG AS HE
KEEPS TRYING.
IT'S WHEN HE STOPS TRYING THAT HE BECOMES
A FAILURE.

SOMETIMES YOU HAVE TO LOOK HARD AT A
PERSON AND REMEMBER...
HE'S JUST TRYING TO GET SOMEPLACE...JUST
LIKE YOU.

BE CAREFUL OF THE WORDS YOU SAY
SO KEEP THEM SOFT AND SWEET.
YOU NEVER KNOW FROM DAY TO DAY
WHICH ONES YOU'LL HAVE TO EAT.

—Marcus Allen

WHAT A MAN IS DEPENDS LARGELY ON WHAT
HE DOES WHEN HE HAS NOTHING TO DO.

THE MAN WITH TIME TO BURN NEVER GAVE THE
WORLD ANY LIGHT.

THE LAZY MAN AIMS AT NOTHING AND
GENERALLY HITS IT.

A TURTLE NEVER MAKES PROGRESS UNTIL HE
STICKS OUT HIS NECK.

IF YOUR WORK SPEAKS FOR ITSELF, THEN DON'T
INTERRUPT IT.

YOU CAN'T FLY WITH THE OWLS AT NIGHT AND
EXPECT
TO SOAR WITH THE EAGLES DURING THE DAY.

THE ONE WHO COMPLAINS ABOUT THE WAY
THE BALL BOUNCES
IS LIKELY THE ONE WHO DROPPED IT.

THE FELLOW WHO BLOWS HIS HORN THE
LOUDEST IS USUALLY
IN THE BIGGEST FOG.

DO NOT LOOK BACK UNLESS YOU PLAN TO GO
THAT WAY.

GOD DOES NOT PROMISE US A TROUBLE-FREE
JOURNEY — ONLY A SAFE ARRIVAL.

"LEAD, FOLLOW, OR GET OUT OF THE WAY."

—George Steinbrenner

IF IT IS TO BE IT IS UP TO ME.

GET THE TIDE UP, AND ALL THE BOATS WILL
RISE.

ASSETS: MAKE THINGS POSSIBLE

PEOPLE: MAKE THINGS HAPPEN

LEARN AS IF YOU WERE TO LIVE FOREVER.
LIVE AS IF YOU WERE TO DIE TOMORROW.

YOU CANNOT LIVE A PERFECT DAY WITHOUT
DOING SOMETHING
FOR SOMEONE WHO WILL NEVER BE ABLE TO
REPAY YOU.

IT'S WHAT YOU LEARN AFTER YOU KNOW IT ALL
THAT COUNTS.

IF YOU DON'T STAND UP FOR SOMETHING,
YOU'LL FALL FOR ANYTHING.

ABILITY MAY GET YOU TO THE TOP, BUT IT TAKES
CHARACTER TO KEEP YOU THERE.

YOU MAY BE AT THE TOP OF THE HEAP, BUT YOU
ARE
STILL PART OF IT.

IF YOU DON'T KNOW WHERE YOU ARE GOING,
YOU'LL END UP SOMEWHERE ELSE.

HAM AND EGGS
CHICKEN IS INVOLVED BUT THE HOG IS
COMMITTED.

MUSCLES DON'T PRODUCE NET PROFIT.

WHEN YOU LAUGH, THE WORLD LAUGHS WITH
YOU;
WHEN YOU CRY, YOU CRY ALONE.

THE HARDER I WORK, THE LUCKIER I GET.

WHY NOT LET THE PEOPLE RUN THE COUNTRY?
RIGHT NOW THE LAWYERS AND POLITICIANS
ARE RUNNING THE COUNTRY.

YOU HAVE NOT FAILED UNTIL YOU START
BLAMING SOMEONE ELSE.

Conclusion

The purpose of Common Sense Management is to bridge the gap between the theory of management and its application. This book strives to help us all be better managers. As we lead and manage, we face many different, complex situations. I hope that after reading and reflecting on this book, when a person confronts one of these situations that by the power of association one of the principles in the book, "Care and Feeding," "Iceberg" will flash into the person's mind and help him determine the best course of action.

Common Sense Management also encourages the notion that most of managing and leading is common sense.

Part III: Readings
"Point of View"

"Point of View"
Work: It Isn't All That Bad

Most of us, for a period of forty years or more, spend about a third of our time working. By this, we usually mean working at some gainful occupation to earn a living or to contribute to family income. However, that time may be spent homemaking, although full-time homemakers are becoming fewer and fewer as wives swell the work force.

As Shakespeare observed, we all pass through different stages in our lives. In each stage, the work ethic takes on a different perspective to us.

The teenager usually takes a dim view of work. In an earlier day, the teenager's contribution was critical to the well-being of the rural American family. Large families were needed to survive in those rugged days. In today's more affluent society, and with family work not available, young people generally do not contribute to the family's economic well-being. However, if the teenager does not have responsibilities, he loses the opportunity to learn to be accountable.

Work has evolved into more of a process of learning, discipline, and pride.

As a person moves into high school and college, work represents an opportunity to earn the means of acquiring what is perceived as "indispensable" needs: a first car, record albums, and extras that dad will not or cannot buy.

When we set out on our careers, work becomes an

extension of ourselves. Success on the job seems to relate to our success as a person. For some reason, one's worth to society seems to be based on one's job. At some point, after we have become somewhat accomplished as an electrician, tool and die maker, college professor, or electrical engineer, we become recognized for our craftsmanship and abilities. Here the work ethic takes on a whole new meaning. Work can become engrossing and something in which we take pride.

During these years, it is vital not to let work become so all-consuming that it distorts our perspective about other aspects of life. Too many people are successful in their careers, but strike out as husbands, wives, fathers, or friends. We must work, but work should not become a devouring monster.

Finally, we phase out of the work force and enter retirement, the years we have looked forward to as "harvest years" of leisure, travel, golf, fishing, etc. But, all too often, disillusionment rears its ugly head. Instead of fulfillment, a sense of deprivation assails us when we are taken from our work. As the retirement age gets lower and lower, more and more of us become susceptible to this problem.

If you hold the view that work is not necessary to your happiness, consider the plight of someone who suddenly becomes unemployed. It is a traumatic, insecure, frightening time. If you are not sure how much you care about your job today, consider how you would feel if you did not have it tomorrow.

If we spend half of our waking hours at work, does it not make sense to put ourselves more wholeheartedly into it? If that much of our waking time is going into that particular activity, our efforts should be the very best we can put forth. Work should be taken as a natural, normal, healthful function and as an opportunity to achieve.

One famous ballplayer said on nationwide television that he loved to play baseball and could not believe he was being paid to do it.

Work might go better for us if we shared his attitude.

[Reprinted by permission of the Tulsa Tribune, 318 South Main Street, Tulsa, Oklahoma, from the September 18, 1978, issue, p. 11 C.]

"Point of View"
Planning Your Life To Be A Winner:

1. The difference between the winner of the PGA Golf Tournament and the tenth-placed player is an average of one stroke; the fiftieth player, only four strokes. You have to be a really good golfer to even be in the top 200, but a margin of only six strokes separates the top from the 200th player.

2. In a study of aerodynamics, one learns that the leading portion of the wing provides most of an airplane's lift. Of all the square feet of space in the plane, only this very small area up and down each wing provides the margin to lift the plane.

3. The launching of a spaceship is an intricate maneuver. Everything has to be exact in terms of the centrifugal force of the earth's movement, the launching speed, and power as the spaceship is thrust into space. The slightest margin of error on the launch will cause the spaceship to be off hundreds of thousand of miles as it goes into orbit.

4. Everyone enjoyed the NCAA basketball championship playoff a few years ago between Georgetown and North Carolina. They played shot-for-shot and point-for-point for forty minutes. With fifteen seconds to go and Georgetown behind by one point, the final play of the game was the margin of difference between being the NCAA champion and finishing in second place.

5. If you study a football game, you will find that five or six key plays made the difference in the game. If

the coaches knew which plays these would be, they would practice all week on those particular plays to be sure they were executed with perfection. The problem is that out of the eighty to one hundred plays executed, one does not know which are the key plays. This forces players to execute all of the plays precisely so that the six or seven are executed properly. The margin for winning boils down to a very few plays.

6. The difference between winning and losing in our lives can be measured by the margin. Whenever the margin play comes along, you will excel and, in the process, become all that you can be.

7. As much as we want to think of something as being glamorous and fascinating, there is always a gritty side we have not seen. The most precious gem was once buried in dirt — and to be truly beautiful — it must be polished and cut and set in the right light. In its original state, it was just as worthy, but its full potential was not known until someone recognized it and was willing and patient enough to set it free. The right amount of polishing is needed so you can realize *your* potential. It is not necessarily what we see on the outside that makes anyone or anything beautiful. It is that glow from the inside. There is always work to be done, a need to keep on refining, polishing, and simplifying.

8. We owe it to ourselves to bring out the best of who we are and, to use our talents for something beautiful and worthy. This requires a staying power that comes only with vision and determination.

9. Here are the essential steps: a) have a vision/dream; b) get the facts, be aware of what is going on around you; c) analyze your strengths and weaknesses; d) make a few assumptions; e) set definite measurable objectives; f) develop a list of strategies for each objective; g) put the plan into action; h) review progress; and i) reward yourself for accomplishment.

"Point of View"
Some Keys To Business Survival

We appear to have reached a point in the chronology of America that has placed both organizational and individual lives in precarious and often crisis positions. Corporations, as well as individuals, are failing and taking bankruptcy. Many people are floundering as they seek new career opportunities and readjust their lives.

Over the past twenty years, I have learned a management philosophy and way of thinking that can provide direction based on observing successful organizations and people in these organizations:

1. Identify the specific needs of the organization in terms of key result areas.

2. Identify specific needs of the persons in the organization. These are usually self-esteem, recognition, and the opportunity for independent thought and action — based on longitudinal surveys we have conducted over the past ten years.

3. Have the organizational team work together, emphasizing the process of planning to determine where the organization wants to be in five years.

4. To determine where it wants to be in five years, the management group must identify purpose, conduct environmental analysis, assess strengths and weaknesses and make assumptions. This creates a written product of their efforts, a plan in writing.

5. After completing assessment of these steps,

both individuals and the group must set specific key objectives for the fifth year.

6. Working back from the fifth year, the organization determines what it wants to accomplish in the fourth, third, second, and first years.

7. If next year's accomplishments do not meet with reality, based on the present situation, then the organization must redefine what is possible next year and work through to the fifth year, seeking compromises each step of the way.

8. Strategies for achieving these objectives must be determined. Every organizational member should have an opportunity to contribute to these strategies.

9. This plan is still considered to be a rough-draft stage until it is presented to whatever is considered the next highest level of management or group to which the management group reports. This gets everything out in the open and is the first step in recognizing the difference between expectations and reality. It is most important that what is to be accomplished, and how, is agreed upon before the task begins.

10. Once the overall five-year plan and strategy are agreed upon, the organization is set to go into action.

11. Operational and action plans are started with an emphasis on breaking down every key result area, making certain persons responsible for the completion of every activity, and clearly defining the authority for every short-term task.

12. A system of reporting success and failure must be determined so that every step from the action steps through the implementation of long-term overall strategies can be identified.

13. Any organizational member should be able to signal a deviation from the plan that requires imme-

diate action to get back on target.

14. A system of intrinsic and extrinsic rewards must be established to reward the organization and provide reinforcement as it goes about the task of getting where it wants to be.

These overall steps will ensure success for an organization or individual. I am continually reminded, and see evidence, that those following this process have met with a large measure of success. It takes hard work, time, and dedication to adhere to a management philosophy and use the strategic planning steps.

The key points are to determine where you want to be in the long term, involve as many people as possible in planning, set targets along the way, provide timely accurate feedback as you progress, and then provide rewards when the right things happen.

[Reprinted from *Tahlequah Daily Press*, Sunday, September 20, 1987, p. 6A.]

"Point of View"
Threads Of Influencing Our Lives

As we journey through life, inevitably we cross the paths of those who have a positive influence on us. In my own life, there were teachers, coaches, relatives, friends in my church, and others who had a positive influence on me.

After a recent fishing trip to Mexico for the famed Lake Guerrero large-mouth bass, I began to see how the concept of the "thread of influence" and bass fishing share something in common. We are "hooked" early in life by positive-influence factors, and a thread follows us all the days of our lives tying us back to those influences.

In many ways, I was like the Guerrero bass on my first leave from basic military service in the summer of 1957. Like the big bass, I had wanted my freedom and joined the military service on my 17th birthday. I had come from a wonderful home with all the love and care that could possibly be lavished on a young, energetic, often unruly, sportsminded teenager. No matter how hard I tried to shake the hook, that thread of influence remained there.

When we were going into the city for our first leave, members of my squadron poured into a tattoo parlor calling me names because I would not follow. As thin as that line of influence was, I could not go in because of the thought of later having to face my parents.

This is not to say there is anything inherently wrong about being tattooed, but it was not right for me.

My parents had planted seeds of influence so that as I made decisions a thousand miles from home, their influence was still there.

As I have progressed through life, many many times the often thin, fragile thread of influence from another person's life has directed me through the temptations and trials that we all face as human beings. This concept of the thread of influence should encourage us all to "hook" as many people around us as we can with loving, positive contributions to their lives, so that they will be inescapably tied to those influences as they live out their years.

At this stage of our lives, each of our children is a real blessing to my wife and to me. For better or worse, they are energetic, independent, and excited about life. Like their father, they have an independent streak. But there is a thread tied to each of their lives, and it will follow them all of their days. It can be a comforting, supporting influence.

The concept is obvious. Those positive, loving, guiding influences are there, and you cannot get loose even if you try. All of us need to examine and acknowledge the threads tied to us by others, and be grateful. Then we should go about the business of tying good, positive threads.

(The Tulsa Tribune, April 2, 1984, reprinted by permission.)

"Point of View"
Twenty Sure Ways To Lose Money

After twenty years of helping people solve business and personal problems, I have discovered a few ways to lose one's hard-earned money. Listen carefully for these phrases, and your objective will soon be attained:

• This opportunity is available for only a short time. . . .

• You have been selected as a winner of a fabulous prize. You must. . . .

• All your friends are in on this. . . .

• You have earned the right, through your success, to be considered for. . . .

• I am a (Christian, member of a lodge or club, and so forth). Do business with me. . . .

Keep talking to the person who uses one of these opening lines and soon he will have — as a popular country song says — the gold mine, and you will have the shaft.

Here are some rules to consider, if your aim is to lose your money quickly:

1. Let someone else, preferably someone you do not know, bring you the investment idea. If they come to your door, by all means, let them in.

2. Constantly worry and plot against paying taxes. Find ways to lose so that you deduct the losses from your taxes.

3. Be a recognized professional with your name in the yellow pages, such as a doctor or a dentist.

4. Be arrogant and have a "godlike" air.

5. Try to get rich quickly.

6. For the ultimate experience, invest money you cannot afford to lose.

7. Respond quickly with action when your mate says, "Why don't you do as well as _____?"

8. Give your mate and children credit cards and no budget.

9. Send your children to college with no account-ability. Provide a car, if possible. Keep them in college no matter what.

10. Use the phone and save those letters, post-cards, and stamps.

11. Buy raw land, the farther away from home the better.

12. Build your wife a bigger closet.

13. Go into a business you know nothing about.

14. Do not develop a personal plan, a financial plan, or set goals.

15. Do not buy insurance of any kind.

16. Do not make out your own personal will. Watch your loved ones from Heaven while they fight over your estate and give most of it to lawyers.

17. Get a divorce.

18. Do a lot of impulse buying.

19. Keep all your money for yourself. Do not give to your church or to any worthy cause.

20. Do not ask for any advice from professionals in

banking, insurance, law, investments, and accounting.

This column is meant to make all of us think before we spend. We all have most likely made some poor economic decisions and learned good lessons. Our quality of life can be affected by our economic decisions. It is to be hoped that we will be more careful and think through how we invest and spend our money.

[Reprinted by permission of The Tulsa Tribune form its August 21, 1987, issue.]

"Point of View"
Our "Rain Forests"
Are Still Shifting

It appears that our present society is facing the same problems dinosaurs faced eons ago.

The dinosaurs were gigantic animals that lived mostly in and around water. Their habitat was rivers and swamps, and they ate soft water plants. Perhaps, over thousands of years, the rain forests shifted, and dinosaurs were unable to adapt to a new environment, which — I am speculating — might have become drier. The dinosaur did not survive and became extinct. Some plants, such as the cactus, and some other animals, such as the smaller lizards, were able to adapt and survive. Still other animals, fish, and birds followed the rain forests and survived.

It appears our society is facing the same kind of shifting that the dinosaurs faced millions of years ago. Some who can continue to live by the same plans and strategies will be able to adapt and survive as the lizard and the cactus did. Other organizations and people will recognize the shift, change and adapt, and keep their activities meeting the needs of people in the mainstream of a shifting world. These organizations and people will prosper.

In northeastern Oklahoma, there are some recognizable trends already:

1) Oil and farm economies continue to decline, 2) tourism is receiving a stronger emphasis, 3) NSU is assuming greater prominence as an educational and

cultural center, 4) people are recognizing that the quality of our water and air must be protected, and 5) the region is becoming a more and more popular retirement area.

All the residents of this area would like to keep things just as they are — the dinosaurs would have preferred the rain forests not to shift. However, we must recognize that this entire exciting, problematical, often frustrating and anxiety-filled world in which we live is experiencing a great wave of change.

We need to acknowledge change and try to adapt as the changes take place. It makes little sense to stay as we are. Past experiences will not be as good a predictor as they have been. It will be of more importance to recognize the rate of change and the direction the world is taking.

[Reprinted by permission of the *Tahlequah Daily Press*, from its Sunday, October 25, 1987, issue.]

"Point of View"
A Look Toward The Year 2000

It is easier to predict that changes of great magnitude will take place from 1885 to the year 2000 than it is to pinpoint when those changes and specific events will take place. A futurist can always say there will be upheavals, highs and lows, political instability, wars and rumors of wars. That is relatively easy because it reflects man and how he has conducted his affairs through the centuries.

But in 1960, few of us would have been able to predict specifically what was going to happen during the years up through 1975. In 1960, would any of us have predicted a presidential assassination, the removal of a president of the United States from office, the rise of the Organization of Petroleum Exporting Countries (OPEC), and staggering inflation? The answer in most cases is no. We knew things were going to change dramatically. We just did not know what the changes would be and when they would take place.

A review of the economic literature shows that in the short term — over the next few years — all sources tend to hover near center stage. Few predict anything dramatic in the way of inflation, interest rates, job shifts, and business activity. If you extended that thought, predictions made only for the next few years would always stay near the center line. And when extended, they would show nothing dramatic happening by the year 2000. That is an inherent weakness in short-term forecasting.

We know that something unpredictable and dramatic is going to take place by the year 2000. So, if nothing else, we must prepare ourselves for handling a dramatic change. The only way I know of to be prepared is to have a very sophisticated long-range planning process in place.

The time and expense of preparing long-range plans will have a payoff when major events take place and an organization leader can bring in his experienced team. He will be able to fine-tune and make orderly changes within a decision framework. The people who will be in trouble are those who manage by "the seat of their pants," who have no idea of where they are or where they are going. When they make the decision that will likely make or break their organizations; they will be taking a shot in the dark.

How do we predict where major events are to happen before the year 2000? The best way to start is to look at basic underlying factors. In the United States, we have rapidly become a service economy. As we lose steelmaking, shipbuilding, and other basic industries, we are setting the stage for an OPEC repeat. Someone is going to take advantage of our weakness and put us in exactly the same position OPEC did in the '70s.

The second area is to look for political uncertainty. There are any number of hot spots, including South Africa, that could create a chain effect that will ripple through to the year 2000.

The third area is economic. You can look at any Economics 101 freshman course and see that there is a series of cycles in economic behavior. Over the next fifteen years, you can count on a major high and a major low. Again, no one can predict when either will happen.

The highs will follow the same pattern as the oil-drilling industry, and the bottom will just fall out with few people seeing the red flags signaling that the change is coming. The key again is the strategic planning system that gets the organization adapting quickly during the upturn and adapting even faster for the downturn.

Peter Drucker, in his article, "The Shape of Industry to Come," contends that demographic and technological change will be the factors having the greatest effect on the future shape of our nation.

If you want to peer into the future and take a look at the year 2000, watch the shape of demographic and technological changes. Count on a few major changes that you will not be able to predict. Have a mindset to be able to cope and react, and it will be an interesting time at the turn of the century. You will not have a really clear picture of the year 2000, but you will be able to see a fuzzy image.

[Reprinted by permission of *The Tulsa Tribune*, from its November 6, 1985, issue.]

About The Author

R. Henry Migliore, Professor of Strategic Planning and Management, Northeastern State University/ University Center at Tulsa. Dr. Migliore teaches at the graduate and undergraduate levels. Formerly Professor of Management and former Dean of the ORU School of Business from 1975 until 1987. He is former manager of the press manufacturing operations of Continental Can Company's Stockyard Plant. Prior to that he was responsible for the industrial engineering function at Continental's Indiana plant. In this capacity, Dr. Migliore was responsible for coordinating the long-range planning process. In addition, he has had various consulting experiences with Fred Rudge & Associates in New York and has served large and small businesses, associations and nonprofit organizations in various capacities. He had made presentations to a wide variety of clubs, groups, and professional associations. Dr. Migliore has been selected to be on the faculty for the International Conferences on Management by Objectives and the Strategic Planning Institute Seminar Series. He is also a frequent contributor to the Academy of Management, including a paper at the 50th anniversary national conference. He served for 12 years on the

Board of Directors of T.D. Williamson, Inc., and was previously on the Boards of the International MBO Institute and Brush Creek Ranch. He is currently on the Board of the American Red Cross/Tulsa Chapter, and is chairman of a scholarship fund for Eastern State College. In 1984 he was elected into the Eastern State College Athletic Hall of Fame. Dr. Migliore has been a guest lecturer on a number of college campuses. He serves on Chamber/Civic Committees, and is on the Administrative Board at The First United Methodist Church, Tulsa, Oklahoma. Recently he was selected Who's Who on a list of 31 top eschelon writers and consultants in America.

To date previous articles on management and business subjects have appeared in *AIIE Journal, Construction News, Management World, Management of Personnel Quarterly, Journal of Long-Range Planning, Dental Economics, Health Care Management Review, MBO Journal, Business and Society Review, Parks and Recreation Journal, The Journal of Business Strategy, Daily Blessing, Ozark Mountaineer, On Line, Real Estate Today, Communication Briefings, Journal of Sports Management,* and the *Planning Review.* His books, *MBO: Blue Collar to Top Executive, An MBO Approach to Long-Range Planning, A Strategic Plan for Your Life, Strategic Long-Range Planning, Strategic Planning for Church and Ministry Growth, Common Sense Management; A Biblical Perspective, Personal Action Planning; How To Know What You Want And Get It,* and *Tales of Uncle Henry,* describe personal theories and experiences. He contributed to the book, *Readings in Interpersonal and Organizational Communication* and *International Handbook on MBO. The Management of Production; A Productivity Approach* is co-authored. *Strategic Management, Strategic Life Planning,* and *Common Sense Management* were published in 1990. He has also produced "Personal Financial Success," an Oral Roberts Ministry video training kit offered on nationwide television, and video/audio tapes to go with his books and a series of video tapes on strategic planning.

In November 1985, the daily "Managing for Success" cable television program was inaugurated and was on the air until March 1986. It was on Tulsa Cable. The series began again on Tulsa Cable in September 1986. He writes occasional columns for the *Tulsa Tribune, Tahlequah Pictorial Press, Collinsville News, Jenks Journal*, and *Muskogee County Times*. A complete video series is available with four summary units and 36 support units.

Dr. Migliore holds degress from Eastern Oklahoma State, Oklahoma State University, St. Louis University, and completed his doctorate at the University of Arkansas. He belongs to the Academy of Management, Planning Executives Institute and is a senior member of the American Institute of Industrial Engineers.

To contact Dr. Migliore,
write:

R. Henry Migliore
P.O. Box 957
Jenks, Oklahoma 74037

Books by
R. Henry Migliore

An MBO Approach to Long-Range Planning

Common Sense Management
An Accountability Approach

Strategic Planning and Management

MBO: Blue Collar To Top Executive

Strategic Long-Range Planning

Tales of Uncle Henry

**Available from your local bookstore
or from:
Managing For Success
P.O. Box 957
Jenks, Oklahoma 74037**

Strategic Planning for Ministry and Church Growth

Common Sense Management
A Biblical Perspective

Personal Action Planning:
How To Know What You Want And Get It

Personal Action Planning
How To Get Where You Are Going In A Hurry

Common Sense Management
An Accountability Approach

Strategic Planning and Management

Production/Operations Management
A Productivity Approach

**Available from:
Nichols/GP Publishing
11 Harts Lane
East Brunswick, NJ 08816**